BEAUTIFUL BAKING AND IRRESISTIBLE TREATS

piece of **cake**

emma summer

southwater

This edition is published by Southwater
Southwater is an imprint of Anness Publishing Ltd
Hermes House, 88–89 Blackfriars Road, London SE1 8HA
tel. 020 7401 2077; fax 020 7633 9499
www.southwaterbooks.com; info@anness.com

UK agent: The Manning Partnership Ltd,
6 The Old Dairy, Melcombe Road, Bath BA2 3LR;
tel. 01225 478444; fax 01225 478440; sales@manning-partnership.co.uk

UK distributor: Grantham Book Services Ltd,
Isaac Newton Way, Alma Park Industrial Estate, Grantham, Lincs NG31 9SD;
tel. 01476 541080; fax 01476 541061; orders@gbs.tbs-ltd.co.uk

North American agent/distributor: National Book Network,
4501 Forbes Boulevard, Suite 200, Lanham, MD 20706;
tel. 301 459 3366; fax 301 429 5746; www.nbnbooks.com

Australian agent/distributor: Pan Macmillan Australia,
Level 18, St Martins Tower, 31 Market St, Sydney, NSW 2000;
tel. 1300 135 113; fax 1300 135 103; customer.service@macmillan.com.au

New Zealand agent/distributor: David Bateman Ltd,
30 Tarndale Grove, Off Bush Road, Albany, Auckland;
tel. (09) 415 7664; fax (09) 415 8892

A CIP catalogue record for this book is available from the British Library.

Publisher: Joanna Lorenz
Senior Cookery Editor: Linda Fraser
Assistant Editor: Emma Brown
Designers: Patrick McLeavey & Jo Brewer
Illustrator: Anna Koska
Photographers: Karl Adamson, Steve Baxter, Amanda Heywood,
Michael Michaels, Don Last & Edward Allright
Recipes: Shirley Gill, Alex Baxter, Christine France, Hilaire Walden, Patricia Lousada,
Norma MacMillan, Roz Denny, Sarah Gates & Elizabeth Wolf-Cohen

Previously published as the *Little Baking Cookbook*

1 3 5 7 9 10 8 6 4 2

Contents

Introduction 6

Biscuits & Bars 12

Teabreads & Muffins 22

Yeast Breads & Rolls 32

Pies & Tarts 42

Cakes & Gâteaux 52

Index 64

Introduction

In an age where so much of what we buy is prepacked, when biscuits come in rolls with tag-pulls for easy opening, freezers are filled with fudge cakes, and ready-to-fill pastry cases are on sale in every supermarket, maybe it is time to campaign for a return to home baking. Remember the smell of newly baked bread, the welcome sight of a batch of fresh scones, the taste of a home-made teabread packed with dried fruits? These are treats few commercial products can match, and if the demands of modern living mean we seldom have time to bake our own biscuits, perhaps we need to look again at how we use the time we have. Baking is one of the most satisfying branches of cookery. Kneading dough can be very therapeutic after a day dealing with difficult clients or demanding children, and the repetitive task of rolling out dough and cutting out cookies can be positively soothing as an antidote to rush hour travel. Much has been made of the dangers of a diet high in fats and sugars. When you do your own baking, you have far more control over what your family eats. Reducing the amount of refined sugar in cakes and biscuits is easy to achieve, especially if you use dried fruits. Low-fat lunch-box treats, like Apricot Yogurt Cookies on page 20, are a much better bet than chocolate bars.

Home baking doesn't have to be horribly time-consuming. Bread is a cinch thanks to easy-blend yeast, which is added directly to the dry ingredients. You can make the dough in a food processor, if you choose, and as it only needs a single proving, baking a loaf of bread or a dozen rolls is simplicity itself.

Many of the cakes and teabreads in this book take very little time to produce, and even pastry, which some people regard as fiddly, is child's play if you remember a few cardinal rules: when you rub fat into flour, work fast and lift the mixture to incorporate air; add only enough liquid to enable the ingredients to bind together; handle the dough as little as possible and roll it out quickly and lightly. Lining pie plates, spooning in filling and adding pastry lids can take time, especially if you crimp the edges and decorate the top of the pie, but there's no need to do any of that if you are in a hurry. Just roll out a large circle to fit the pie plate with plenty of overlap, add your filling and lop the extra pastry over. It won't cover the filling completely but that doesn't matter – the rustic effect is part of the charm. The Open Apple Pie on page 47 is made by this method and very good it is too.

For special occasions try some of the more elaborate cakes like the Chocolate Fudge Gâteau on page 54 or the Raspberry & Hazelnut Meringue Cake on page 56. Either of these would make a stunning and delicious centrepiece for a celebration tea or a fitting finale to a special dinner party.

Baking Ingredients

SUGAR

Caster sugar is the type most commonly used because it dissolves faster and gives a lighter result. Brown sugar is favoured for its flavour in fruit cakes.

DRIED FRUIT

An invaluable storecupboard ingredient, dried fruit is sold ready-cleaned and seeded for cakes and desserts.

NUTS

Buy nuts only when you need them if possible, as they can become rancid if kept too long. Opened packets can be stored in the fridge or freezer.

BAKING POWDER

Made from bicarbonate of soda, selected acids and starch, this is an effective raising agent, and is added to plain flour.

BICARBONATE OF SODA

This raising agent produces a rapid rise in the presence of an acid. Cakes containing bicarbonate of soda should be baked as soon as possible after mixing.

FLOUR

Most of the recipes in this book use plain, strong or self-raising white flour. Where sifted wholemeal flour is stipulated, return the bran from the sieve to the bowl.

EGGS

Unless recipes specify otherwise, use size 3 eggs. Keep them point-downwards in their box in the fridge, allowing them to come to room temperature before use. Always buy eggs from a reputable supplier.

BUTTER

For rich cakes and pastries, butter is the fat of choice. Two types are available – sweet cream butter and lactic butter, the latter tasting slightly more acidic.

MARGARINE

For most cake mixtures, margarine gives good results. Bring block margarine to room temperature before creaming, but use soft margarine straight from the fridge.

OILS

Choose light oils with no discernible flavour for baking. Sunflower oil is ideal, but groundnut oil or vegetable oil are also fine for most baking purposes.

YEAST

Breads and some cakes use yeast as the raising agent. The development of easy-blend yeast has revolutionized home baking because it is so quick and simple to use, although some cooks still prefer to bake with fresh yeast. A third kind of yeast, active dried yeast, has now largely been replaced by easy-blend yeast.

Baking Techniques

KNEADING

Working yeast dough by folding it towards you, then pushing it down and away with the heel of one or both hands. The dough is turned and the action repeated, often for several minutes, until it feels elastic and no longer sticky.

FOLDING

Lightly mixing an aerated ingredient such as whisked egg whites into other ingredients so that the air does not escape. A metal spoon or a rubber spatula is used with a very light up-and-over action, turning the bowl as you work.

CREAMING

Beating together softened fats with sugar, using a wooden spoon or electric whisk, to make a mixture that resembles whipped cream.

RUBBING-IN

The diced fat (usually butter) is added to the flour, then rubbed between the fingertips until the mixture resembles breadcrumbs.

PROVING

Putting the dough in a covered bowl (or the baking tin), covering and setting aside in a warm place, such as an airing cupboard, until doubled in bulk.

LINING A ROUND TIN

Draw two circles on greaseproof or non-stick baking paper to fit the bottom of the tin and cut out. Then cut a long strip slightly longer than the circumference of the tin and about 5cm/2in taller. Crease the paper strip about 2.5cm/1in from a long side, then snip the paper diagonally at intervals from edge to fold. Grease the tin lightly with oil, fit one of the paper circles in the bottom, then fit the long strip around the inside with the snipped fringe overlapping neatly at the bottom. Brush lightly with oil, then fit the second paper circle in place at the bottom of the tin.

LINING A SQUARE TIN

Cut a piece of greaseproof or non-stick baking paper big enough to cover the bottom of the tin and come up the sides, adding an extra 2.5cm/1in all round. Centre the tin on the paper, then make four cuts in from the side of the paper to the corners of the tin. Overlap the corners of the paper to construct a box the same shape as the tin. Grease the tin and fit the lining in place.

TIME-SAVING TIP

Freeze appropriate amounts of rubbed-in mixture. Thaw when needed and use for cakes, pastries or crumble toppings. Add sugar and spice as required.

Biscuits & Bars

Chocolate Nut Cookies

INGREDIENTS

25g/1oz plain chocolate, broken into squares
25g/1oz bitter cooking chocolate,
broken into squares
225g/8oz/2 cups plain flour
2.5ml/½ tsp salt
225g/8oz/1 cup unsalted butter,
at room temperature
225g/8oz/1 cup caster sugar
2 eggs, beaten
5ml/1 tsp vanilla essence
115g/4oz/1 cup walnuts, finely chopped

MAKES 50

1 Combine the plain and bitter chocolate squares in a heatproof bowl. Bring a small saucepan of water to the boil, remove from the heat and place the bowl on top. Set aside until the chocolate has completely melted, then stir until smooth. Sift the flour and salt into a small bowl; set aside.

2 Using an electric mixer, cream the butter in a mixing bowl until soft. Add the sugar and beat until light and fluffy. Beat in the eggs and vanilla essence, a little at a time, then stir in the melted chocolate. Add the flour mixture and the nuts and fold in gently until well mixed together.

13

3 Divide the mixture equally into four parts, and, with your hands, roll each into a log, about 5cm/2in in diameter. Wrap each chocolate log tightly in foil and  chill overnight in the fridge, or place the logs in the freezer for several hours until firm.

4 Preheat the oven to 190°C/375°F/Gas 5. Grease two or three baking sheets. With a sharp knife, cut the logs into 5mm/¼in slices. Place the rounds on the baking sheets and bake for 10 minutes or until lightly coloured. Cool on wire racks.

Florentines

INGREDIENTS

40g / 1 1/2oz / 3 tbsp unsalted butter
120ml / 4fl oz / 1/2 cup whipping cream
115g / 4oz / 1/2 cup caster sugar
115g / 4oz / 1 cup flaked almonds
50g / 2oz / 1/3 cup chopped mixed peel
40g / 1 1/2oz / 1/4 cup glacé cherries, chopped
65g / 2 1/2oz / generous 1/2 cup plain flour, sifted
225g / 8oz plain chocolate, broken into squares
5ml / 1 tsp sunflower oil

MAKES ABOUT 36

1 Preheat the oven to 180°C/350°F/Gas 4. Grease two baking sheets. Melt the butter, cream and sugar in a saucepan, then bring to the boil. Remove from the heat and mix in the almonds, peel, cherries and flour.

2 Drop small spoonfuls of the mixture 5cm/2in apart on the prepared baking sheets. Flatten with a fork. Bake for 10 minutes or until the florentines start to colour at the edges. Remove from the oven and quickly neaten the edges with a knife or round biscuit cutter. Use a metal palette knife to transfer the florentines to a clean, flat surface.

3 Melt the chocolate in a bowl over hot water. Add the oil and stir until well blended. Use the palette knife to spread the smooth underside of the cooked flo-

rentines with a thin coating of melted chocolate. Arrange on a rack and leave until almost set.

4 Draw a serrated knife across the surface of the chocolate, using a very slight sawing action, to make wavy lines. Allow to set completely before serving.

COOK'S TIP

When tidying the edges on the freshly cooked florentines, try to work fast, or they will harden on the baking sheets. If necessary, return them to the oven for a few minutes to soften.

Chocolate-tipped Hazelnut Crescents

INGREDIENTS

225g/8oz/2 cups plain flour
pinch of salt
225g/8oz/1 cup unsalted butter, softened
50g/2oz/¼ cup caster sugar
15ml/1 tbsp hazelnut liqueur or water
5ml/1 tsp vanilla essence
425g/15oz milk chocolate
50g/2oz/½ cup roasted chopped hazelnuts
icing sugar, for dusting

MAKES ABOUT 35

1 Preheat the oven to 160°C/325°F/Gas 3. Grease two large baking sheets. Sift the flour and salt together into a bowl and set aside.

2 Using an electric mixer, cream the butter in a mixing bowl. Add the sugar and beat until fluffy, then beat in the hazelnut liqueur or water and vanilla essence. Gently stir in the flour mixture, until just blended. Set aside 350g/12oz of the chocolate and grate the rest into the mixture. Add the chopped hazelnuts and fold in lightly.

3 With very light-ly floured hands, shape the dough into about 35 5 x 1cm/2 x ½in crescents. Place on the baking sheets, 5cm/2in apart. Bake for about  20–25 minutes until golden. Cool on the baking sheets for 10 minutes, then use a palette knife to transfer to wire racks to cool completely.

4 Line the clean baking sheets with non-stick baking paper. Dust the crescents with icing sugar. Melt the remaining chocolate in a bowl over hot water. Using tongs, dip half of each crescent into the chocolate, place on the prepared baking sheets and chill until the chocolate has set.

Easter Biscuits

INGREDIENTS

*115g/4oz/½ cup unsalted butter
or margarine
90ml/6 tbsp caster sugar, plus extra
for sprinkling
1 egg, separated
200g/7oz/1¾ cups plain flour
2.5ml/½ tsp mixed spice
2.5ml/½ tsp ground cinnamon
50g/2oz/⅓ cup currants
15ml/1 tbsp chopped mixed peel
15-30ml/1-2 tbsp milk*

MAKES 16—18

1 Preheat the oven to 200°C/400°F/Gas 6. Lightly grease two baking sheets. Cream the butter or margarine with the caster sugar until light and fluffy, then beat in the egg yolk. Sift the flour and spices over the egg mixture, then fold in with the currants and mixed peel, adding enough of the milk to make a fairly soft dough.

2 Turn the dough on to a floured surface, knead lightly until just smooth, then roll out to a thickness of about 5mm/¼in. Cut into rounds, using a 5cm/2in fluted biscuit cutter. Space the rounds on the prepared baking sheets and bake for 10 minutes.

3 Beat the egg white in a small bowl. Remove the biscuits from the oven, brush them immediately with the egg white and sprinkle with extra caster sugar. Return to the oven and bake for about 10 minutes more, until golden. Leave to cool on wire racks.

17

Pecan Bars

INGREDIENTS

225g/8oz/2 cups plain flour
pinch of salt
115g/4oz/½ cup caster sugar
115g/4oz/½ cup unsalted butter
or margarine
1 egg
finely grated rind of 1 lemon
TOPPING
175g/6oz/¾ cup unsalted butter
60ml/4 tbsp clear honey
50g/2oz/¼ cup sugar
150g/5oz/scant 1 cup soft dark brown sugar
75ml/5 tbsp whipping cream
450g/1lb/4 cups pecan nuts, halved

MAKES 36

1 Preheat the oven to 190°C/375°F/Gas 5. Lightly grease a 41 x 26cm/15½ x 10½in Swiss roll tin. Sift the flour and salt into a mixing bowl. Stir in the sugar. Add the butter or margarine and cut in with a knife, then rub in until the mixture resembles coarse breadcrumbs.

2 Add the egg and lemon rind and mix with a fork until the mixture just holds to-gether. Spoon the mixture into the prepared tin, then press it out evenly. Prick all over with a fork and leave to chill in the fridge for about 10 minutes.

3 Bake the dough base for 15 min-utes, then remove from the oven while you make the topping. Keep the oven on. Melt the butter, honey and both sugars in a saucepan. Bring to the boil and boil without stirring for 2 minutes. Remove from the heat and stir in the cream and pecan nuts. Pour the mixture over the dough base, return the tin to the oven and bake for 25 minutes more. Cool in the tin.

4 Run a knife around the edge of the dough. Invert on to a clean baking sheet, then place another sheet on top and invert again. Dip a sharp knife into very hot water and cut into squares for serving.

18

Apricot Yogurt Cookies

INGREDIENTS

175g/6oz/1½ cups plain flour
5ml/1 tsp baking powder
5ml/1 tsp ground cinnamon
75g/3oz/1 cup rolled oats
75g/3oz/½ cup soft light brown sugar
115g/4oz/⅔ cup ready-to-eat dried apricots
15ml/1 tbsp flaked hazelnuts or almonds
150ml/¼ pint/⅔ cup natural yogurt, plus
extra yogurt or milk (see method)
45ml/3 tbsp sunflower oil
demerara sugar, to sprinkle

MAKES 16

1 Preheat the oven to 190°C/375°F/ Gas 5. Lightly grease a large baking sheet with oil. Sift together the plain flour, baking powder and cinnamon into a large mixing bowl. Using a wooden spoon stir in the oats, light brown sugar, dried apricots and nuts.

2 In a small bowl, whisk the yogurt and oil together. Pour into the flour mixture and mix to a firm dough. If necessary, add a little extra yogurt or milk.

3 With floured hands, form the mixture into 16 rough mounds. Place them on the baking sheet, leaving room for spreading, then flatten with a fork. Sprinkle with sugar and bake for 15–20 minutes. Cool for 5 minutes, then transfer to a wire rack.

COOK'S TIP

These cookies do not keep very well, so it is best to eat them within 2 days, or freeze them. Open freeze, pack in polythene bags, label and freeze for up to 4 months.

Teabreads & Muffins

Apricot Nut Loaf

INGREDIENTS

115g/4oz/⅔ cup dried apricots
1 large orange
75g/3oz/½ cup raisins
150g/5oz/⅔ cup caster sugar
90ml/6 tbsp sunflower oil
2 eggs, lightly beaten
250g/9oz/2¼ cups plain flour
10ml/2 tsp baking powder
2.5ml/½ tsp salt
5ml/1 tsp bicarbonate of soda
50g/2oz/½ cup chopped walnuts
butter, to serve

MAKES 1 LOAF

1 Line a 23 x 13cm/9 x 5in loaf tin with grease-proof paper. Grease the paper. Place the apricots in a bowl, cover with warm water and leave to stand for about 30 minutes.

2 Preheat the oven to 180°C/350°F/Gas 4. Pare the orange thinly and cut the rind into thin match-sticks. Squeeze the pared orange and add water, if necessary, to make 175ml/6fl oz/¾ cup.

3 Drain the apricots and cut into small pieces. Mix the orange rind, apricots and raisins in a bowl and pour over the orange juice. Mix together well. Stir in the sugar, oil and eggs.

4 In a separate bowl, sift together the flour, baking powder, salt and the bicarbonate of soda. Fold into the apricot mixture in three batches. Stir in the walnuts.

5 Spoon the mixture into the prepared tin and bake for 55–60 minutes or until a skewer inserted in the loaf comes out clean. Leave the loaf to cool in the tin for 10 minutes, then transfer to a rack and leave to cool completely. Serve with butter.

Banana & Orange Teabread

INGREDIENTS

75g / 3oz / ¾ cup wholemeal flour
75g / 3oz / ¾ cup plain flour
5ml / 1 tsp baking powder
5ml / 1 tsp mixed spice
45ml / 3 tbsp flaked hazelnuts, toasted
2 large ripe bananas
1 egg
30ml / 2 tbsp sunflower oil
30ml / 2 tbsp clear honey
finely grated rind and juice of 1 small orange
DECORATION
4 orange slices, halved
10ml / 2 tsp icing sugar

MAKES 1 LOAF

I Preheat the oven to 180°C/350°F/ Gas 4. Line the base of a 23 x 13cm/9 x 5in loaf tin with grease-proof paper. Grease the paper with a small amount of oil. Sift together the flours, baking powder and mixed spice into a mixing bowl, adding any bran that remains in the sieve. Stir in the hazelnuts. Mix until all ingredients are thoroughly combined.

2 Mash both of the bananas in a mixing bowl with a fork. Beat in the egg, sunflower oil, honey, orange rind and juice. Add to the dry ingredients and mix well.

Spoon the banana mixture into the prepared loaf tin and smooth down the top with a knife or with the back of a spoon.

3 Bake for 40–45 minutes, or until firm and golden brown. Turn out on to a wire rack. Leave to cool until required. Preheat the grill.

4 Sprinkle the orange slices with the icing sugar. Place them on a rack over a grill pan and grill until golden, taking care not to let them burn. Cool slightly, then arrange the slices on top of the loaf.

COOK'S TIP

If you plan to keep the loaf for more than two to three days, omit the orange slices and brush the warm loaf with honey instead. Sprinkle with flaked hazelnuts, if you like.

Sticky Gingerbread

INGREDIENTS

175g/6oz/1½ cups plain flour
10ml/2 tsp ground ginger
2.5ml/½ tsp mixed spice
2.5ml/½ tsp bicarbonate of soda
30ml/2 tbsp black treacle
30ml/2 tbsp golden syrup
75g/3oz/½ cup soft dark brown sugar
75g/3oz/⅓ cup unsalted butter
1 egg
15ml/1 tbsp milk
15ml/1 tbsp orange juice
2 pieces of preserved stem ginger, finely chopped
50g/2oz/⅓ cup sultanas
5 ready-to-eat dried apricots, finely chopped
45ml/3 tbsp icing sugar
10ml/2 tsp lemon juice

MAKES 1 LOAF

1 Preheat the oven to 160°C/325°F/Gas 3. Line a 23 x 13cm/9 x 5in loaf tin with greaseproof paper. Grease the paper. Sift the flour, spices and bicarbonate of soda into a mixing bowl.

2 Combine the black treacle, golden syrup, soft dark brown sugar and unsalted butter in a heavy-based saucepan. Heat gently, stirring, until the butter has melted and the sugar has dissolved. Take care not to overcook or the mixture will burn. Cool slightly.

3 In a small bowl, whisk the egg, milk and orange juice together. Add to the dry ingredients, together with the syrup mixture and the ginger, sultanas and apricots. Mix well. Spoon into the prepared tin, level the surface and bake for 50 minutes or until the gingerbread is well risen and a skewer inserted in the loaf comes out clean.

4 Cool the gingerbread in the tin for 10 minutes, then remove from the tin and cool completely on a wire rack. Beat the icing sugar and lemon juice together in a small bowl until smooth. Drizzle over the top of the gingerbread, leave to set, then cut into thick slices to serve.

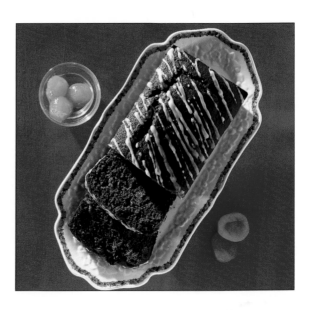

Pineapple & Apricot Teabread

INGREDIENTS

225g / 8oz / 2 cups plain flour
1.5ml / ¼ tsp salt
7.5ml / 1½ tsp baking powder
175g / 6oz / ¾ cup unsalted butter
150g / 5oz / ⅔ cup caster sugar
3 eggs, beaten
few drops of vanilla essence
115g / 4oz / ⅔ cup crystallized pineapple, chopped
115g / 4oz / ⅔ cup crystallized ginger, chopped
225g / 8oz / 1⅓ cups ready-to-eat dried apricots, chopped
grated rind and juice of ½ orange
grated rind and juice of ½ lemon
milk (see method)

MAKES I LOAF

1 Preheat the oven to 180°C/350°F/Gas 4. Line an 18cm/7in square cake tin with greaseproof paper. Grease the paper. Sift the flour, salt and baking powder into a bowl.

2 Cream the butter and sugar together in a mixing bowl until pale and fluffy. Gradually add the beaten eggs, beating well after each addition, and adding a little of the flour mixture if the mixture shows signs of curdling. Beat in the vanilla essence, then fold in half of the remaining flour mixture.

3 Fold in the pineapple, ginger, apricots and grated citrus rind, with the rest of the flour. Add enough of the citrus juice to give a fairly soft dropping consistency. (Add a little milk if necessary). Spoon into the prepared tin and level the top.

4 Bake for 20 minutes, then lower the oven temperature to 160°C/325°F/Gas 3 and bake for 1–1¼ hours more, until firm. Cool for 10 minutes in the tin, then turn out on a wire rack to cool.

Dried Cherry Muffins

28

INGREDIENTS

250ml/8fl oz/1 cup natural yogurt
175g/6oz/1 cup dried cherries
115g/4oz/½ cup butter, at room temperature
175g/6oz/¾ cup caster sugar
2 eggs
5ml/1 tsp vanilla essence
200g/7oz/1¾ cups plain flour
10ml/2 tsp baking powder
5ml/1 tsp bicarbonate of soda
pinch of salt

MAKES 16

1 In a mixing bowl, combine the yogurt and cherries. Cover and leave to stand for 30 minutes.

2 Preheat the oven to 180°C/350°F/Gas 4. Grease a 16-cup bun tin or arrange 16 double paper cake cases on baking sheets.

3 With an electric mixer, cream the butter and sugar together until light and fluffy.

4 Add the eggs, one at a time, beating well after each addition. Add the vanilla essence and the cherry mixture and stir to blend. Set aside.

5 In another bowl, sift together the flour, baking powder, bicarbonate of soda and salt. Fold into the cherry mixture in three batches.

6 Fill the prepared cups two-thirds full. Bake for about 20 minutes, until the tops spring back when touched lightly. Transfer to a wire rack to cool.

Chocolate Chip Muffins

INGREDIENTS

*115g / 4oz / ½ cup unsalted butter
or margarine
65g / 2½oz / generous ¼ cup caster sugar
30ml / 2 tbsp soft dark brown sugar
2 eggs, beaten
175g / 6oz / 1½ cups plain flour
5ml / 1 tsp baking powder
120ml / 4fl oz / ½ cup milk
175g / 6oz / 1 cup chocolate chips*

MAKES 10

3 Divide half the mixture between 10 muffin cups or cases and sprinkle the chocolate chips over, then cover with the remaining mixture. Bake for 20–25 minutes, or

until the muffins are well risen. The tops of the muffins should spring back when lightly touched. If paper cases were not used, cool in the cups for 5 minutes before turning out. Serve warm or cool.

1 Preheat the oven to 190°C/375°F/ Gas 5. Lightly grease a 12-cup muffin tin, or use paper cases. Using an electric mixer, cream together the unsalted butter or margarine with the caster and soft dark brown sugar until light and fluffy. Beat in the eggs, a little at a time, adding a small amount of flour if the mixture shows signs of curdling.

2 Sift the flour and baking powder into a separate bowl. Fold into the creamed mixture in stages, alternately with the milk.

29

Apple & Cranberry Muffins

INGREDIENTS

150g/5oz/1¼ cups plain flour
5ml/1 tsp baking powder
2.5ml/½ tsp bicarbonate of soda
5ml/1 tsp ground cinnamon
2.5ml/½ tsp grated nutmeg
2.5ml/½ tsp ground allspice
1.5ml/¼ tsp ground ginger
1.5ml/¼ tsp salt
50g/2oz/¼ cup unsalted butter or margarine
1 egg, beaten
90ml/6 tbsp caster sugar
grated rind of 1 large orange
*120ml/4fl oz/½ cup freshly squeezed
orange juice*
1-2 eating apples
115g/4oz/1 cup cranberries
50g/2oz/½ cup chopped walnuts
icing sugar, for dusting

MAKES 12

30

1 Preheat the oven to 180°C/350°F/Gas 4. Lightly grease a 12-cup muffin tin. Sift the flour, baking powder, bicarbonate of soda, spices and salt into a large bowl. Melt the butter or margarine.

2 Whisk together the beaten egg and melted butter or margarine. Add the sugar, orange rind and juice, and mix together well.

3 Peel, quarter, and core the apples, then chop coarsely. Make a well in the centre of the dry ingredients and pour in the egg mixture. With a large metal spoon, stir for just long enough to moisten the flour – the mixture need not be smooth.

4 Fold the apples, cranberries and walnuts into the mixture. Spoon the mixture into the muffin cups, filling them three-quarters full. Bake for 25–30 minutes until the muffins are well risen. The tops should spring back when lightly touched. Cool in the cups for 5 minutes before turning out. Serve warm or cool, dusted with icing sugar.

Yeast Breads
& Rolls

Poppy Seed Knots

INGREDIENTS

350ml / 12fl oz / 1½ cups milk
50g / 2oz / ¼ cup unsalted butter
675g / 1½lb / 6 cups strong white flour
10ml / 2 tsp salt
10g / ¼oz sachet easy-blend dried yeast
1 egg yolk
1 egg, to glaze
10ml / 2 tsp water
poppy seeds (see method)

MAKES 18

1 Heat the milk and butter in a saucepan, stirring occasionally, until the butter has melted. Pour into a jug and cool to hand-hot.

2 Sift the flour and salt into a bowl. Stir in the yeast. Make a well in the centre and add the milk mixture and the egg yolk. Mix to a soft dough. Knead on a lightly floured surface for about 10 minutes, until smooth and elastic but not sticky.

3 Grease a large baking sheet. Divide the dough into 18 pieces, about the size of golf balls. Roll each piece into a rope and twist to form a knot. Place the knots 2.5cm / 1in apart on the baking sheet. Cover loosely and leave to rise in a warm place until the knots have doubled in size.

4 Preheat the oven to 230°C/450°F/ Gas 8. Beat the egg with the water in a cup. Brush the glaze over the knots and sprinkle with the poppy seeds. Bake for 12–15

minutes or until the tops of the knots are lightly browned. Transfer the knots to a rack and leave to cool slightly before serving warm.

Clover Leaf Rolls

INGREDIENTS

300ml / ½ pint / 1¼ cups milk
50g / 2oz / ¼ cup unsalted butter
450g–500g / 1–1¼lb / 4–5 cups strong
white flour
10ml / 2 tsp salt
30ml / 2 tbsp caster sugar
10g / ¼oz sachet easy-blend dried yeast
1 egg, beaten
melted butter, for glazing

MAKES 24

1 Place the milk and butter in a saucepan and heat, stirring occasionally, until the butter has melted. Pour into a jug and cool to hand-hot.

2 Sift 450g/1lb/ 4 cups of the flour with the salt into a large bowl. Stir in the sugar and yeast. Make a well in the centre, add the milk and but-ter mixture, then add the beaten egg. Mix to a rough dough, adding more flour if necessary. Knead on a lightly floured surface for about 10 minutes, until the dough is smooth, elastic and no longer sticky.

3 Grease two 12-cup bun tins with a small amount of oil. Divide the dough into four equal pieces and, with your hands, roll each piece to a rope about 35cm/

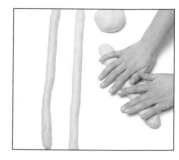

14in long. Cut each rope into about 18 pieces and form each piece into a small ball.

4 Place three of the balls, side by side, in each bun cup. Cover loosely and leave to rise in a warm place until almost doubled in size. Meanwhile, preheat the oven

to 230°C/450°F/Gas 8. Brush the rolls lightly with melted butter to glaze. Bake for about 12–15 minutes or until lightly browned. Cool slightly on a rack before serving.

34

Multi-grain Bread

INGREDIENTS

65g/2½oz/generous ¾ cup rolled oats
600ml/1 pint/2½ cups milk
60ml/4 tbsp sunflower oil
60g/2oz/⅓ cup soft light brown sugar
30ml/2 tbsp clear honey
450g/1lb/4 cups strong white flour
175g/6oz/2 cups soya flour
350g/12oz/3 cups wholemeal flour
25g/1oz/½ cup wheatgerm
10ml/2 tsp salt
2 x 10g/¼oz sachets easy-blend dried yeast
2 eggs, lightly beaten

MAKES 2 LOAVES

I Place the oats in a large bowl. In a saucepan, bring the milk to just below boiling point. Pour the hot milk over the oats, then stir in the oil, sugar and honey.

2 Allow the oat mixture to cool. Combine the flours, wheatgerm, salt and yeast in a large mixing bowl. Add the oat mixture and eggs and mix to a rough dough. Knead on a lightly floured surface for about 10 minutes, until smooth and elastic.

3 Grease two 23 x 13cm/9 x 5in loaf tins. Divide the dough into four equal pieces and roll each to a rope slightly longer than the tin and about 4cm/1½in thick. Twist the ropes together in pairs and place in the tins. Cover loosely and leave to rise in a warm place until doubled in size.

4 Preheat the oven to 220°C/425°F/ Gas 7. Bake the loaves for about 30–35 minutes or until the bottoms of each loaf sound hollow when they are lightly tapped. (Tap the bottoms of both the loaves by clenching your hand together to make a fist and hold the top of the loaf with your other hand.) Cool on a rack.

Danish Wreath

INGREDIENTS

175ml/6fl oz/¾ cup milk
450g/1lb/4 cups strong white flour
2.5ml/½ tsp salt
50g/2oz/¼ cup caster sugar
10g/¼oz sachet easy-blend dried yeast
2.5ml/½ tsp vanilla essence
1 egg, beaten
2 x 115g/4oz blocks of unsalted butter
1 egg yolk
10ml/2 tsp water
chopped pecan nuts or walnuts, for sprinkling
FILLING
*200g/7oz/generous 1 cup soft dark
brown sugar*
5ml/1 tsp ground cinnamon
*50g/2oz/½ cup pecan nuts or walnuts,
toasted and chopped*
ICING
115g/4oz/¾ cup icing sugar
a little water

SERVES 10–12

1 Heat the milk until hand-hot. Sift the flour and salt into a bowl. Stir in the sugar and yeast. Make a well and add the milk, vanilla essence and egg. Mix to a rough dough. Knead on a lightly floured surface for 10 minutes, until smooth and elastic. Wrap and chill for 15 minutes.

2 Place each block of butter between two sheets of greaseproof paper. Flatten each with a rolling pin to a 15 x 10cm/6 x 4in rectangle.

3 Roll out the dough to a 30 x 20cm/12 x 8in rectangle. Place one butter rectangle in the centre, fold the bottom third of dough over and seal the edge. Place the second butter rectangle on top and cover with the top third of the dough. Roll out to the original size and fold into thirds. Wrap in clear film and chill for 30 minutes.

4 Repeat the rolling, folding and chilling twice more, then chill for 1–2 hours. Stir the filling ingredients together.

5 Grease a baking sheet. Roll out the dough to a 63 x 15cm/25 x 6in strip. Spread the filling over it, leaving a 1cm/½in border. Roll up lengthways into a cylinder. Form into a circle on the baking sheet, pinching the edges together to seal. Cover and leave to rise for 45 minutes.

6 Preheat the oven to 200°C/400°F/Gas 6. Slash the top of the wreath with a knife, at regular intervals. Beat together the egg yolk and water and brush over the wreath. Bake for 35–40 minutes. Cool on a wire rack. Meanwhile, make a thin icing by mixing the icing sugar with a little water. When the wreath is cold, decorate it by spooning over the icing and sprinkling with the chopped nuts.

Cinnamon & Walnut Yeast Cake

INGREDIENTS

900g / 2lb / 8 cups strong white flour
10ml / 2 tsp salt
50g / 2oz / ¼ cup caster sugar
30ml / 2 tbsp easy-blend dried yeast
350ml / 12fl oz / 1½ cups milk
120ml / 4fl oz / ½ cup water
165g / 5½oz / generous ¾ cup
unsalted butter
2 eggs, beaten
7.5ml / 1½ tsp grated orange rind
175g / 6oz / 1¼ cups icing sugar
45-60ml / 3-4 tbsp orange juice
FILLING
90g / 3½oz / scant ½ cup caster sugar
50g / 2oz / ½ cup walnuts, finely chopped
7.5ml / 1½ tsp ground cinnamon

MAKES 2 CAKES

1 Sift the flour and salt into a large bowl. Stir in the sugar and yeast. Heat the milk and water with half the butter in a saucepan until the butter has melted. Pour into a jug and cool to hand-hot.

2 Make a well in the centre of the dry ingredients and add the eggs, grated orange rind and the milk mixture. Mix, gradually incorporating the surrounding flour to make a soft dough. If necessary, add a little more flour.

3 Knead the dough on a lightly floured surface for about 10 minutes, until it is smooth, elastic and no longer sticky.

4 Mix the filling ingredients in a bowl. Grease two 25cm/10in round cake tins. Knead the dough lightly and divide it in half. On a lightly floured surface, roll out one piece to a 30 x 20cm/12 x 8in rectangle. Melt the remaining butter. Brush half the butter over the dough and set the rest aside. Sprinkle over half the filling, roll up tightly from a long side and pinch the seam to seal it.

5 With a sharp knife, cut the roll across in 2.5cm/ 1in slices. Arrange the slices, cut side down, in the prepared tins. Repeat the process with the rest of the  dough, melted butter and filling. Cover both tins and leave the dough to rise in a warm place until the dough slices have almost doubled in size. Preheat the oven to 190°C/375°F/Gas 5.

6 Bake the cakes for about 30–35 minutes or until golden. Cool on a wire rack. Decorate by mixing the icing sugar with enough orange juice to make a thin icing. Drizzle over the cakes and leave to set.

40

Pies & Tarts

Walnut & Pear Lattice Pie

INGREDIENTS

225g/8oz/2 cups plain flour
1.5ml/¼ tsp salt
115g/4oz/½ cup chilled butter, diced
25g/1oz/¼ cup finely chopped walnuts
45-60ml/3-4 tbsp iced water
50g/2oz/⅓ cup icing sugar
15ml/1 tbsp lemon juice
FILLING
900g/2lb pears
50g/2oz/¼ cup caster sugar
60ml/4 tbsp plain flour
2.5ml/½ tsp grated lemon rind
45ml/3 tbsp raisins or sultanas
45ml/3 tbsp chopped walnuts
2.5ml/½ tsp ground cinnamon

SERVES 6–8

1 Sift the flour and salt together into a mixing bowl. Rub in the butter and stir in the walnuts and enough iced water to moisten. Gather into a ball, wrap and chill for 30 minutes. Preheat the oven to 190°C/375°F/Gas 5.

2 Make the filling. Peel the pears and slice into a bowl. Add the caster sugar, flour and rind. Toss to coat the fruit. Add the raisins or sultanas, walnuts and cinnamon. Mix lightly.

3 Roll out half the pastry on a lightly floured surface and line a 23cm/9in pie tin that is about 5cm/2in deep. Roll out the remaining pastry to a 28cm/11in round and cut it into 1cm/½in wide strips. Spoon the filling into the pastry case. Arrange the pastry strips on top, carefully weaving them in and out to make a lattice. Bake for about 55 minutes or until golden.

4 Combine the icing sugar, lemon juice and 5–10ml/1–2 tsp cold water in a bowl. Mix until smooth. Remove the pie from the oven, drizzle over the icing then leave to cool slightly before serving.

43

Red Berry Tart with Lemon Cream Filling

INGREDIENTS

150g / 5oz / 1¼ cups plain flour
25g / 1oz / ¼ cup cornflour
45ml / 3 tbsp icing sugar
90g / 3½oz / scant ½ cup chilled unsalted
butter, diced
2 egg yolks
5ml / 1 tsp vanilla essence
sprig of mint, to decorate
FILLING
200g / 7oz / scant 1 cup cream cheese, softened
45ml / 3 tbsp lemon curd
grated rind and juice of 1 lemon
icing sugar (see method)
225g / 8oz / 2 cups mixed red berry fruits
45ml / 3 tbsp redcurrant jelly

SERVES 6—8

1 Sift the flour, cornflour and icing sugar into a bowl. Rub in the butter until the mixture resembles breadcrumbs. (This can be done in a food processor). Beat the egg yolks with the vanilla essence in a cup. Add to the dry ingredients and mix to a firm dough, adding a little cold water if necessary.

2 Roll the pastry out into a round and use to line a 23cm/9in flan tin, pressing the pastry well up the sides after trimming. Prick the base all over with a fork. Chill for 30 minutes. Line the pastry case with greaseproof paper and fill with baking beans.

3 Preheat the oven to 200°C/400°F/Gas 6. Place the pastry case on a baking sheet and bake for 20 minutes, removing the paper and beans for the last 5 minutes. Cool, then remove the pastry case from the tin and place on a serving plate.

4 Cream together the cheese, lemon curd, lemon rind and lemon juice, adding icing sugar to sweeten, if liked. Spread the mixture in the pastry case and then arrange the mixed berries on top. Warm the redcurrant jelly in a saucepan, sieve it, then trickle or brush it over the fruit. Decorate the tart with a sprig of mint and serve at once.

Plum Pie

INGREDIENTS

275g/10oz/2½ cups plain flour
5ml/1 tsp salt
75g/3oz/⅓ cup chilled unsalted butter
50g/2oz/½ cup chilled vegetable fat or lard
60-120ml/4-8 tbsp iced water
milk, for glazing
FILLING
900g/2lb red or purple plums,
halved and stoned
grated rind of 1 lemon
15ml/1 tbsp lemon juice
115-175g/4-6oz/½-¾ cup caster sugar
45ml/3 tbsp quick-cooking tapioca
pinch of salt
2.5ml/½ tsp ground cinnamon
1.5ml/¼ tsp grated nutmeg

SERVES 8

1 Sift the flour and salt into a bowl. Rub in the butter and vegetable fat or lard until the mixture resembles breadcrumbs. Stir in just enough iced water to bind the pastry. Gather into two balls, one slightly larger than the other. Wrap and chill for 20 minutes.

2 Preheat the oven to 220°C/425°F/Gas 7. Line a baking sheet with greaseproof paper. Set it aside. Roll out the larger piece of pastry to a thickness of about 3mm/⅛in and line a 23cm/9in pie dish.

3 Roll out the smaller piece of pastry to a round slightly larger than the top of the pie. Support it on the prepared baking sheet, then stamp out four hearts from the centre of the pastry, using a cutter. Reserve the pastry hearts.

4 Make the filling by mixing all the ingredients in a bowl. Use the larger quantity of sugar if the plums are very tart. Spoon the filling into the pastry case, then lift the pastry on the greaseproof paper and slide it into position over the filling. Trim and pinch to seal. Arrange the cut-out pastry hearts on top. Glaze the top of the pie with milk and bake for 15 minutes. Lower the oven temperature to 180°C/350°F/Gas 4 and bake for 30–35 minutes more, protecting the top with foil if needed.

Open Apple Pie

INGREDIENTS

275g/10oz/2½ cups plain flour
2.5ml/½ tsp salt
115g/4oz/½ cup chilled unsalted
butter, diced
50g/2oz/¼ cup chilled vegetable fat, diced
75-90ml/5-6 tbsp iced water
FILLING
1.5kg/3lb sweet-tart firm eating or
cooking apples
50g/2oz/¼ cup sugar
10ml/2 tsp ground cinnamon
grated rind and juice of 1 lemon
25g/1oz/2 tbsp butter, diced
30-45ml/2-3 tbsp clear honey

SERVES 8

1 Sift the flour and salt together into a mixing bowl. Rub in the butter and vegetable fat until the mixture resembles coarse breadcrumbs. Stir in just enough iced water to moisten the dry ingredients, then gather together to make a ball. Wrap the pastry and chill for 30 minutes.

2 Preheat the oven to 200°C/400°F/Gas 6. Very lightly grease a deep 23cm/9in pie dish and set aside. Peel, quarter and core the apples, then slice them into a bowl. Add the sugar, cinnamon, lemon rind and juice and toss together well.

3 Roll out the pastry on a lightly floured surface to a 30cm/12in round. Place the pastry over the pie dish so that the excess dough overhangs the edges. Fill with the apple mixture, then fold in the pastry edges, crimping them loosely to make a decorative border. Dot the apples with the diced butter.

4 Bake the pie for about 45 minutes, until the pastry is golden and the apples are tender. Melt the honey in a saucepan. Remove the pie from the oven and immediately brush the honey over the apples to glaze. Serve warm or at room temperature.

47

Mince Pies

INGREDIENTS

450g/1lb/4 cups plain flour
150g/5oz/1 cup icing sugar
350g/12oz/1½ cups chilled unsalted
butter, diced
grated rind and juice of 1 orange
milk, for glazing
icing sugar, for dusting
FILLING
175g/6oz/¾ cup blanched almonds, very
finely chopped
150g/5oz/scant 1 cup dried apricots,
finely chopped
175g/6oz/1 cup raisins
150g/5oz/scant 1 cup currants
150g/5oz/scant 1 cup glacé cherries
150g/5oz/scant 1 cup chopped mixed peel
115g/4oz/¾ cup suet
grated rind and juice of 2 lemons
grated rind and juice of 1 orange
200g/7oz/generous 1 cup soft dark brown sugar
4 cooking apples
10ml/2 tsp ground cinnamon
5ml/1 tsp grated nutmeg
2.5ml/½ tsp ground cloves
250ml/8fl oz/1 cup brandy
225g/8oz/1 cup cream cheese
30ml/2 tbsp caster sugar

MAKES 36

1 Make the filling. Mix the nuts, dried and preserved fruit, suet, citrus rind and juice and brown sugar in a large bowl. Quarter, core and peel the apples. Chop them finely or grate them, and add them to the bowl with the spices. Stir in the brandy. Cover the mincemeat and set aside in a cool place for a couple of days to mature.

2 To make the pastry, sift the flour and icing sugar into a bowl. Rub in the butter until the mixture resembles breadcrumbs. Add the orange rind. Stir in just enough orange juice to moisten, then gather into a ball. Wrap and chill for 30 minutes.

3 Preheat the oven to 230°C/450°F/Gas 8. Beat together the cream cheese and caster sugar. Roll out just over half the pastry on a lightly floured surface to a thickness of 3mm/⅛in. Using a 7.5cm/3in fluted cutter, stamp out 36 rounds. Fit the rounds in bun trays. Half fill each with mincemeat and top with 5ml/1 tsp of the cream cheese mixture.

4 Roll out the remaining pastry and use a 5cm/2in cutter to stamp out 36 lids. Brush the edges of the filled pastry cases with milk, then set the rounds on top. Cut a small steam vent in the top of each.

5 Glaze the pies lightly with milk. Bake for about 15–20 minutes, until golden. Cool for 10 minutes before easing out on to a wire rack. Serve warm or at room temperature, dusted with icing sugar.

Iced Strawberry Pie

INGREDIENTS

115g / 4oz sweetmeal biscuits, crushed
15ml / 1 tbsp caster sugar
65g / 2½oz / 5 tbsp unsalted butter, melted
225g / 8oz / 1 cup cream cheese, softened
250ml / 8fl oz / 1 cup soured cream
500g / 1¼lb / 5 cups strawberries,
thawed if frozen

SERVES 8

1 Make the base by mixing the crushed biscuits and sugar with the melted butter in a bowl, stirring well to combine. Press the biscuit crumb mixture evenly over the bottom and sides of a 23cm/9in pie dish, then freeze until the biscuit case is firm.

2 Beat the cream cheese in a bowl with a wooden spoon. Gradually add the soured cream, beating the mixture until it is smooth. Slice the strawberries. Set aside a quarter of them for the topping; fold the rest into the mixture. Pour the filling into the biscuit case and freeze for 6–8 hours until firm.

3 To serve, cut the pie into slices and spoon over some of the reserved strawberries, with a little of their juice.

Chocolate Cheesecake Pie

INGREDIENTS

350g/12oz/1½ cups cream cheese, softened
60ml/4 tbsp double cream
225g/8oz/1 cup caster sugar
50g/2oz/½ cup cocoa powder
2.5ml/½ tsp ground cinnamon
3 eggs
BASE
75g/3oz sweetmeal biscuits, crushed
45g/1½oz amaretti (or extra sweetmeal
biscuits), crushed
75g/3oz/⅓ cup unsalted butter, melted
DECORATION
whipped cream
chocolate curls

SERVES 8

1 Preheat the oven to 180°C/350°F/Gas 4. Make the base by mixing the crushed biscuits with the melted butter. Press the mixture evenly over the bottom and sides of a 23cm/9in pie dish. Bake for 8 minutes, then cool. Leave the oven on, and put a baking sheet inside to heat.

2 Beat the cheese and cream in a bowl with an electric mixer until smooth. Beat in the sugar, cocoa and cinnamon until blended, then add the eggs, one at a time, beating for just long enough to combine. Pour the filling into the biscuit case and bake on the hot baking sheet for 25–30 minutes. The filling will sink as the cheesecake cools. Decorate with whipped cream and chocolate curls when cold.

Cakes & Gâteaux

American Carrot Cake

INGREDIENTS

250ml/8fl oz/1 cup sunflower oil
175g/6oz/¾ cup sugar
3 eggs
175g/6oz/1½ cups plain flour
7.5ml/1½ tsp baking powder
7.5ml/1½ tsp bicarbonate of soda
1.5ml/¼ tsp salt
7.5ml/1½ tsp ground cinnamon
1.5ml/¼ tsp grated nutmeg
1.5ml/¼ tsp ground ginger
115g/4oz/1 cup chopped walnuts
2 large carrots, finely grated
5ml/1 tsp vanilla essence
30ml/2 tbsp soured cream
8 tiny marzipan carrots, to decorate
FROSTING
175g/6oz/¾ cup full fat soft cheese
25g/1oz/2 tbsp unsalted butter, softened
250g/9oz/2 cups icing sugar

SERVES 8

1 Preheat the oven to 180°C/350°F/Gas 4. Base-line and grease two 20cm/8in cake tins. Beat the oil and sugar together and add the eggs, one at a time, beating well after each addition. Sift the flour, baking powder, bicarbonate of soda, salt and spices into the bowl. Beat well, then stir in the walnuts, carrots, vanilla essence and soured cream.

2 Divide the mixture between the prepared tins. Bake for 40–50 minutes or until well risen and springy to the touch. Cool the cake layers in their tins on a wire rack.

3 Meanwhile make the frosting. Beat together the soft cheese, butter and icing sugar, using a wooden spoon, until smooth.

4 Sandwich the cake layers together with a little of the frosting. Spread the rest over the top and sides of the cake, using a round-bladed knife to make a swirling pattern. Decorate the cake with the tiny marzipan carrots just before serving.

Chocolate Fudge Gâteau

INGREDIENTS

225g/8oz plain chocolate, chopped
115g/4oz/½ cup unsalted butter, diced
150ml/¼ pint/⅔ cup water
225g/8oz/1 cup caster sugar
10ml/2 tsp vanilla essence
2 eggs, separated
150ml/¼ pint/⅔ cup soured cream
275g/10oz/2½ cups plain flour
10ml/2 tsp baking powder
5ml/1 tsp bicarbonate of soda
pinch of cream of tartar
chocolate curls, raspberries and icing sugar,
to decorate
CHOCOLATE FUDGE FILLING
450g/1lb plain chocolate, chopped
225g/8oz/1 cup unsalted butter
75ml/5 tbsp brandy
225g/8oz/¾ cup seedless raspberry preserve
GANACHE
250ml/8fl oz/1 cup double cream
225g/8oz plain chocolate, chopped
30ml/2 tbsp brandy

SERVES 18–20

1 Preheat the oven to 180°C/350°F/Gas 4. Base-line and grease a 25cm/10in springform cake tin. Place the chocolate, butter and water in a saucepan. Heat gently, until melted.

2 Pour into a large bowl and beat in the sugar and vanilla essence. Leave to cool, then beat in the egg yolks. Fold in the soured cream. Sift the dry ingredients then fold them into the mixture. Whisk the egg whites in a bowl until stiff and gently fold in.

3 Pour the mixture into the prepared tin. Bake for 45–50 minutes. Leave to cool for 10 minutes then remove from the tin, place on a wire rack and leave to cool completely. Wash and dry the tin.

4 Make the fudge filling. Gently melt the chocolate and butter with 60ml/4 tbsp of brandy. Set aside to cool. Meanwhile, cut the cake into three layers. Heat the preserve with the remaining brandy and spread over each cake layer. Leave to set.

5 Return the bottom layer to the tin, spread with half the filling, top with the middle cake layer and spread over the remaining filling. Add the top cake layer and press down gently. Chill overnight.

6 Make the ganache. Bring the cream to the boil, remove from the heat and stir in the chocolate, then the brandy. Strain, then set aside for 5 minutes to thicken. Remove the cake from its tin and pour the ganache over the top, smoothing down over the sides to cover. Pipe any remaining ganache around the base of the cake using a star-shaped nozzle. When set, decorate with chocolate curls, raspberries and icing sugar. Do not chill the glazed cake.

Raspberry & Hazelnut Meringue Cake

INGREDIENTS

4 egg whites
225g/8oz/1 cup caster sugar
few drops of vanilla essence
5ml/1 tsp malt vinegar
115g/4oz/1 cup roasted chopped
hazelnuts, ground
300ml/½ pint/1¼ cups double cream
350g/12 oz/3 cups raspberries
icing sugar, for dusting
mint sprigs, to decorate
SAUCE
225g/8oz/2 cups raspberries
45-60ml/3-4 tbsp icing sugar
15ml/1 tbsp orange liqueur

SERVES 6

1 Preheat the oven to 180°C/350°F/ Gas 4. Base-line and grease two 20cm/8in sandwich cake tins. Whisk the egg whites in a bowl until stiff peaks  form. Gradually whisk in the caster sugar. When stiff, gently fold in the vanilla, vinegar and nuts.

2 Divide the mixture between the prepared tins and bake for 50–60 minutes, or until crisp. Remove gently from the tins and leave to cool on a wire rack.

3 Make the sauce. Purée the raspberries with the icing sugar and liqueur in a food processor or blender. Press through a fine sieve into a jug. Chill until ready to serve.

4 In a bowl, whip the cream to soft peaks. Gently fold in the raspberries. Place one round of meringue on a serving plate and spread the raspberry and cream  mixture evenly over the top. Place the second round of meringue on top to form a sandwich.

5 Dust the top of the gâteau liberally with icing sugar and decorate with mint sprigs. Serve with the raspberry sauce. (To cut the gâteau, use a large and very sharp knife.)

Chocolate Cream Cake

INGREDIENTS

175g/6oz/¾ cup soft margarine
115g/4oz/½ cup caster sugar
60ml/4 tbsp golden syrup
175g/6oz/1½ cups self-raising flour, sifted
2.5ml/½ tsp salt
45ml/3 tbsp cocoa powder, sifted
3 eggs, beaten
15-30ml/1-2 tbsp milk (optional)
150ml/¼ pint/⅔ cup whipping cream
15-30ml/1-2 tbsp fine-shred marmalade
icing sugar, for dusting

SERVES 8–10

1 Preheat the oven to 180°C/350°F/ Gas 4. Base-line and grease two 18cm/7in sandwich cake tins. Combine the margarine, sugar and syrup, flour, salt, cocoa, and eggs in a bowl. Beat the mixture until smooth, or use a food processor fitted with a plastic blade, using the slowest speed. Beat in enough milk to give a soft dropping consistency. Divide the mixture between the tins and spread evenly.

2 Bake the cake layers for 30 minutes or until the tops are just firm and the cakes are springy to the touch. Cool in the tins for 5 minutes, then invert the cake layers on wire racks to cool completely.

3 Whip the cream in a bowl until it holds soft peaks, then gently fold in the marmalade. Reserving the best cake layer for the top, sandwich the layers together with the flavoured cream. Dust the cake with icing sugar and transfer to a serving plate.

Blueberry Cup Cakes

INGREDIENTS

115g/4oz/½ cup soft margarine
115g/4oz/½ cup caster sugar
5ml/1 tsp grated lemon rind
2 eggs, beaten
115g/4oz/1 cup self-raising flour, sifted
pinch of salt
120ml/4fl oz/½ cup whipping cream
75-115g/3-4oz/¾-1 cup blueberries
icing sugar, for dusting

MAKES 12–14

1 Preheat the oven to 190°C/375°F/Gas 5. Grease a 12-cup bun tin or arrange 12–14 double paper cake cases on baking sheets.

2 Cream together the margarine and sugar in a large bowl until pale and fluffy, then stir in the lemon rind. Beat in the eggs, a little at a time, then fold in the  flour and salt, until well mixed. Divide the mixture between the bun tin or paper cake cases. Bake for 15–20 minutes, until golden. Cool on a wire rack.

3 Using a small, sharp-pointed knife, carefully cut out a circle of sponge from the top of each cake. Set these sponge circles aside until required.

4 Whip the cream in a bowl. Place a spoonful of cream on each cup cake, add 2–3 blueberries and replace the sponge lids at an angle. Sift icing sugar over the top of each cup cake.

Orange & Apricot Roulade

INGREDIENTS

4 egg whites
115g/4oz/½ cup golden caster sugar
50g/2oz/½ cup plain flour
finely grated rind of 1 small orange
45ml/3 tbsp orange juice
icing sugar, for dusting
shreds of pared orange rind, to decorate
FILLING
115g/4oz/⅔ cup ready-to-eat dried apricots
150ml/¼ pint/⅔ cup orange juice

SERVES 6

1 Preheat the oven to 200°C/400°F/Gas 6. Grease a 33 x 23cm/13 x 9in Swiss roll tin and line it with non-stick baking paper. Grease the paper. Whisk the egg whites in a grease-free bowl until soft peaks form. Gradually add the sugar, whisking hard after each addition, then gently fold in the flour, orange rind and juice.

2 Spoon the mixture into the prepared Swiss roll tin and spread it evenly. Bake for 15–18 minutes, or until the sponge is firm and pale golden in colour. Turn out on to a sheet of non-stick baking paper. Working quickly, roll up the sponge loosely from one short side and leave the roll to cool.

3 Make the filling. Roughly chop the apricots and place them in a saucepan with the orange juice. Bring to simmering point, cover and cook until most of the liquid has been absorbed. Purée the apricots in a food processor or blender. Cool.

4 Carefully unroll the roulade and spread evenly with the apricot purée. Roll up again and transfer to a platter. Arrange paper strips diagonally across the roll, sprinkle it lightly with icing sugar, then carefully remove the paper to create the patterned effect. Decorate the roll with orange rind and serve.

White Chocolate & Strawberry Gâteau

INGREDIENTS

115g/4oz fine quality white chocolate, chopped
120ml/4fl oz/½ cup double cream
120ml/4fl oz/½ cup milk
15ml/1 tbsp rum or vanilla essence
115g/4oz/½ cup unsalted butter, softened
175g/6oz/¾ cup caster sugar
3 eggs
225g/8oz/2 cups plain flour
5ml/1 tsp baking powder
pinch of salt
675g/1½lb/6 cups strawberries, sliced,
plus extra for decorating
750ml/1¼ pints/3 cups whipping cream
30ml/2 tbsp rum
WHITE CHOCOLATE MOUSSE FILLING
250g/9oz fine quality white chocolate, chopped
350ml/12fl oz/1½ cups whipping or
double cream
30ml/2 tbsp rum

SERVES 10

1 Preheat the oven to 180°C/350°F/Gas 4. Grease and flour two 23cm/9in round cake tins, about 5cm/2in deep. Base-line the tins with non-stick baking paper. Melt the chocolate in the cream in a double boiler over low heat, stirring until smooth. Stir in the milk and rum or vanilla essence. Set aside to cool.

2 Cream the butter and sugar until fluffy. Beat in the eggs one at a time. Sift together the flour, baking powder and salt and add to the egg mixture in batches, alternately with the melted chocolate, until just blended.

3 Divide the mixture between the prepared tins. Bake for 20–25 minutes or until a skewer inserted in the centre of each cake layer comes out clean. Cool in the tins for 10 minutes, then turn out on to wire racks, peel off the baking paper and leave to cool completely.

4 Make the filling. Melt the chocolate with the cream in a saucepan over low heat, stirring frequently. Stir in the rum and pour into a bowl. Chill until just set, then whip the mixture lightly until it has a mousse-like consistency.

5 Slice each cake layer in half horizontally to make four layers. Spread a third of the mousse on top of one layer and arrange a third of the strawberries over the mousse. Place another cake layer on top of the first and cover with mousse and strawberries as before. Repeat this process once more, then top with the final cake layer.

6 Whip the cream with the rum. Spread about half the flavoured cream over the top and sides of the cake. Use the remaining cream and strawberries to decorate the cake as desired.

Index

American carrot cake, 53
Apples: apple & cranberry
    muffins, 30
  open apple pie, 47
Apricots: apricot nut loaf, 23
  apricot yogurt cookies, 20
  pineapple & apricot
    teabread, 27

Banana & orange teabread, 24
Blueberry cup cakes, 59
Bread: clover leaf rolls, 34
  Danish wreath, 38
  multi-grain bread, 36
  poppy seed knots, 33

Cakes: American carrot
    cake, 53
  chocolate cream cake, 58
  chocolate fudge gâteau, 54
  orange & apricot
    roulade, 60
  raspberry & hazelnut meringue
    cake, 56
  white chocolate & strawberry
    gâteau, 62
Carrots: American carrot
    cake, 53
Cheesecake: chocolate cheesecake
    pie, 51
Cherries: dried cherry muffins, 28
Chocolate: chocolate cheesecake
    pie, 51
  chocolate chip muffins, 29
  chocolate cream cake, 58
  chocolate fudge gâteau, 54

chocolate nut cookies, 13
chocolate-tipped hazelnut
    crescents, 16
Cinnamon & walnut yeast
    cake, 40
Clover leaf rolls, 34
Cranberries: apple & cranberry
    muffins, 30

Danish wreath, 38

Easter biscuits, 17

Florentines, 14
Fruit: red berry tart with lemon
    cream filling, 44

Gingerbread, sticky, 26

Hazelnuts: chocolate-tipped hazelnut
    crescents, 16
  raspberry & hazelnut meringue
    cake, 56

Lemons: red berry tart with lemon
    cream filling, 44

Mince pies, 48
Muffins: apple & cranberry
    muffins, 30
  chocolate chip muffins, 29
  dried cherry muffins, 28

Multi-grain bread, 36

Pears: walnut & pear lattice pie, 43
Pecan bars, 18
Pies and tarts: chocolate cheesecake
    pie, 51
  iced strawberry pie, 50
  mince pies, 48
  open apple pie, 47
  plum pie, 46
  red berry tart with lemon cream
    filling, 44
  walnut & pear lattice pie, 43
Pineapple & apricot teabread, 27
Plum pie, 46
Poppy seed knots, 33

Raspberries: raspberry & hazelnut
    meringue cake, 56

Sticky gingerbread, 26
Strawberries: iced strawberry
    pie, 50

Teabreads: banana & orange
    teabread, 24
  pineapple & apricot teabread, 27

Walnuts: apricot nut loaf, 23
  chocolate nut cookies, 13
  cinnamon & walnut yeast
    cake, 40
  walnut & pear lattice pie, 43

Yogurt: apricot yogurt
    cookies, 20